Hibiscus

First published in 1986 by
David Bateman Limited, 32-34 View Road
Glenfield, Auckland, New Zealand

ISBN 0-908610-46-7

Printed in Hong Kong by Colorcraft Ltd

Other books by Catherine Hamilton
Butterflies of New Zealand
Fiji, The Garden Isles
Hamilton is a Garden
England is a Garden
Alison Holst's Cookery Notes
Australian Year Book
New Zealand Address Book
New Zealand Birthday Book

The New Zealand Year Book

Illustrated by
Catherine Hamilton

Jasmine

BATEMAN
New Zealand

Days to Remember

New Year's Day	January 1
Public Holiday	January 2
Southland Anniversary Day	January 17
Wellington Anniversary Day	January 22
Auckland Anniversary Day	January 29
Nelson Anniversary Day	February 1
Waitangi Day	February 6
St Valentine's Day	February 14
St David's Day	March 1
St Patrick's Day	March 17
Otago Anniversary Day	March 23
Taranaki Anniversary Day	March 31
April Fool's Day	April 1
Queen Elizabeth's Birthday	April 21

Pennyroyal

Carnation

Days to Remember

St George's Day	April 23
Anzac Day	April 25
May Day	May 1
Labour Day	4th Monday in October
Halloween	October 31
Hawkes Bay Anniversary Day	November 1
Marlborough Anniversary Day	November 4
Chathams Anniversary Day	November 30
Westland Anniversary Day	December 1
Canterbury Anniversary Day	December 16
Christmas Day.	December 25
Boxing Day	December 26
New Year's Eve	December 31

Red Rose

The original paintings by Catherine Hamilton reproduced in this book are for sale. Further information can be obtained by sending a stamped addressed envelope to the publisher.

January

1

2

3

4

5

6

7

Marjoram

Raspberry

January

8

9

10

11

12

January

13

14

15

16

17

18

19

Capsicum

January

20

21

22

23

24

Strawberry

January

25

26

27

28

29

Borage

30

31

Notes

Passionfruit

February

1

2

3

4

Chervil

5

6

7

February

8

9

10

Plums

February

11

12

Maidenhair fern

13

14

15

16

17

February

18

19

20

21

22

23

24

Vanilla Flowers

February

25

26

27

28

29

Honeysuckle

Notes

Comfrey

Flannel Flower

March

1

2

3

4

5

6

March

7

8

9

10

11

12

13

Water lilies

March

14

15

16

17

18

19

20

Lavender

March

21

22

23

24

25

26

27

Black Protea

March

28

29

30

31

Geranium

Notes

Caper buds

April

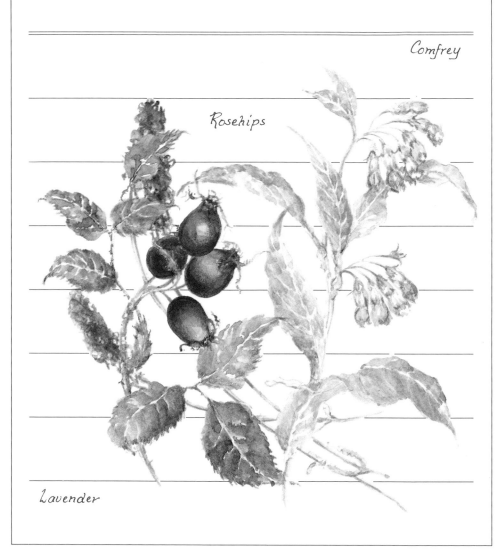

Comfrey

Rosehips

Lavender

April

1

2

3

4

5

6

White Butterfly

April

7

8

9

10

11

12

13

Parsley

April

14

15

16

17

18

19

Mushrooms

April

20

21

22

Chrysanthemum

23

24

25

26

27

28

29

30

Virginia Creeper

Notes

Tussock Butterfly

Notes

Bird's Nest Fern

Boston Fern

May

Mint

Blackberry

Ground Ivy

Sage

Crab Apple

May

Bell Fruited Gum Flowers

1

2

3

4

5

6

7

May

8

9

10

11

12

13

14

Autumn Snowflake

May

Crab Apples

15

16

17

18

19

May

20

21

22

23

24

25

26

Macadamia Nuts

May

27

28

29

30

31

Poinsettia

Notes

Crepe Myrtle leaves

Notes

Paris Daisy

June

Camellias

June

June

1

2

3

4

5

6

7

Salad Burnet

June

8

9

10

11

12

13

14

Gypsophila

June

15

16

17

18

19

Sage

Sage and Bee

June

20

21

22

23

24

25

26

June

27

28

29

30

Forget-me-Not

Notes

July

Poppies

Sweet Pea

Chrysanthemum

Bougainvillea

July

1

2

3

4

Cyclamen

July

5

6

7

8

Hedgehog

July

9

10

11

12

13

14

15

Haka - N.Z. Violet

July

Fernbird

16

17

18

19

20

July

21

22

23

24

25

Fernbird.

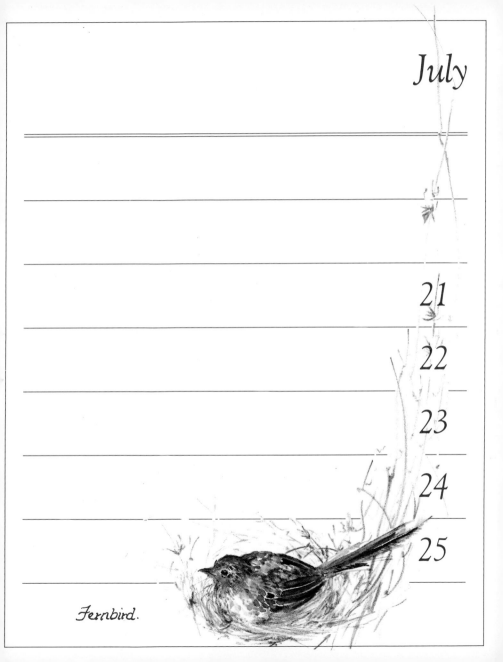

July

26

27

28

29

30

31

Rock Wren

Notes

Acorns

August

Feijoa.

1

2

3

4

August

5

6

7

8

Sand Convolvulus

August

9

10

11

12

13

14

Miro Drupes

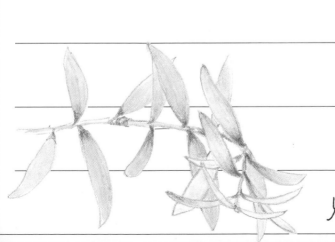

August

15

16

17

18

19

Young Kauri leaves

August

20

21

22

23

24

Little Spotted Kiwi

August

Koru Berries

25

26

27

28

29

30

31

Notes

White Kaka Beak

Notes

Maori Onion

September

Variegated Fairy Wren

September

Apple blossom

1

2

3

4

September

5

6

7

8

9

10

11

Camphor

September

12

13

14

15

16

17

18

Jonquil

September

_____

_____

_____

19

Rhododendron. Elizabeth Hobbie

20 2006 - Sealing 9 patio blocks + new rep 9 blocks

21

22

23

September

_____

24

_____
'06   BEDROOM MIRRORS

25

_____

26

_____

27

_____

28

_____
S'HEET

29

_____

30

_____

Iris

Notes

Tulip

Thyme

Notes

October

Chrysanthemum

Paris Da

October

Poppies

Jonquil

October

Violets

1

2

3

4

5

October

6

7

8

9

10

11

Wheat.

12

October

13

14

15

16

Daffodils and Daisies

17

18

October

19

20

21

22

23

Fledgling Sparrow

October

24

25 *White Clover*

26

27

October

28

29

30

31

Sand Sedge

November

Bottlebrush

Wattle

November

1

2

3

4

Bougainvillea

November

5

6

7

8

9

10

11

Wallflower

November

12

13

14

15

French Marigold

November

28

29

30

Mimulus

Notes

Day Lily

December

Pascali Rose

December

Primula

Lasiandra

1

2

3

December

Gladiolus

4

5

6

7

8

9

10

December

11

12

13

14

15

16

17

Azalea

December

Field Rose

18

19

20

21

December

22

23

24

25

Dog Rose

December

26

27

28

29

30

31

Hibiscus

Notes

Hydrangea,

Notes

Spearmint